Force & Moti

MW00353645

Grades 1-3

Written by Sandra Appleby
Illustrated by Keith Milne

ISBN 1-55035-707-7
Copyright 2003
Revised January 2006
All Rights Reserved * Printed in Canada

Published in the United States by:
On the Mark Press
3909 Witmer Road PMB 175
Niagara Falls, New York
14305
www.onthemarkpress.com

Published in Canada by:
S&S Learning Materials
15 Dairy Avenue
Napanee, Ontario
K7R 1M4
www.sslearning.com

Look For OTHER SCIENCE UNITS

FORCE & MOTION

Table of Contents

Table of Contents (cont'd)

Objectives:

Understanding Basic Concepts

The students will:
1. Identify force as a push or pull by one body on another.
2. Investigate the ways in which different forces (e.g., magnetism, static electricity, muscular force, gravitational force) can change the speed or direction of a moving object.
3. Investigate the effect of magnets and electrically charged objects on the motion of different materials (e.g., iron filings will be moved by a magnet, whereas grains of sugar will not).
4. Identify, through observation, different forms of energy and suggest how they might be used to provide power to devices and to create movement (e.g., the release of energy from a tightly wound rubber band or spring would create movement in a wind-up toy).
5. Distinguish between kinds of motion and indicate whether the motions were caused indirectly (e.g., by gravity, static electricity, magnets) or directly (e.g., by applied force).
6. Investigate the effects of directional forces (e.g., left push for left movement) and how unbalanced forces can cause visible motion in objects that are capable of movement (e.g., an object pushed over a smooth floor).

Developing Skills of Inquiry, Design and Communication

The students will:
1. Ask questions about and identify needs and problems related to the behaviour of different forces in their immediate environment, and explore possible answers and solutions (e.g. identify everyday situations that produce static electricity and describe ways of removing static electricity from clothes; compare the strength of two magnets in holding layers of paper on a refrigerator door, or in picking up paper clips).
2. Plan investigations to answer some of these questions or solve some of these problems, and explain the steps involved.
3. Use appropriate vocabulary in describing their investigations, explorations, and observations (e.g., use terms such as push, pull, load, distance, and speed when describing the effect of forces on an object).
4. Record relevant observations, findings, and measurements, using written language, draw in, charts, and graphs (e.g., track a toy boat moving on water at various speeds, record the distances travelled, and present their findings on a chart.
5. Communicate the procedures and results of investigations for specific purposes and to specific audiences, using drawings, demonstrations, simple media works, and oral and written descriptions (e.g., give a demonstration showing how a device has been constructed and how it performs; make a drawing showing what alterations would be made to its design in the future; describe in writing the steps they used to build a device).
6. Design and construct a device that uses a specific form of energy in order to move (e.g., a paper airplane propelled by hand).

Relating Science and Technology to the world Outside the School

The students will:
1. Describe the visible effects of forces acting on a variety of everyday objects (e.g., a toy car goes forward when pushed; a ball falls down when dropped).
2. Identify surfaces that affect the movement of objects by increasing or reducing friction (e.g., dry roads, icy roads).
3. Demonstrate how a magnet works and identify ways in which magnets are useful (e.g., as metal detectors, as a car wrecker's hoist, as a power source for magnetic trains).
4. Recognize devices that are controlled automatically (e.g., a remote–control toy), or by hand (e.g., the flushing mechanism on a toilet).
5. Identify parts of systems used in everyday life, and explain how the parts work together to perform a specific function (e.g., a subway system, a plant, a wind-up toy).

Teacher Suggestions

- The teacher needs to be familiar with the various kinds of forces and how they impact on motion.

- A review of the scientific method for the students and teacher would be useful.

- Try any experiments in advance that will be attempted with the students.

- Plan the unit based on the objectives to be met, moving from objectives to evaluation to activity.

- Encourage the students to explore and question the world around them.

- Collect all materials required prior to starting the unit.

- Plan for modifications to meet individual student needs.

- Discuss and practice safety rules and procedures in the science laboratory.

- Use as many examples from the students' experiences as possible.

- Encourage students to formulate their own questions and experiments on the topic.

Bibliography

Reid, Clare and Paul, <u>Taking off With Flight Grades 1-3;</u> P &C Edcon, 1999

Reid, Clare and Paul, <u>Learning About Simple Machines Grades 1-3;</u> P &C Econ, 1999

Vancleave, Janice, <u>Physics for Every Kid;</u> John Wiley and Sons, 1991

Murphy, Bryan, <u>Experiment with Movement;</u> Two-Can Publishing, Princeton, NJ, 2001

Graham, John, <u>Hands On Science: Forces and Motion;</u> Kingfisher, New York, New York, 2001

Scientific Method

The scientific method is a set of rules that scientists use when approaching a problem they are trying to solve.

1 Think about what you want to know and ask a **question.**

2 **Predict** what you think the answer to this question is!

- before you begin your experiment, guess what the outcome will be by writing it down;
- this is called your hypothesis.

3 **Plan/Procedures**

- design an experiment that will answer your question;
- gather all of the equipment that you need in order to perform the experiment;
- make a list of all the things you will need to do for your experiment.

4 **Observe**

- as you complete the steps of your experiment, record all your observations.

5 **Conclusion**

- after you've completed the experiment, write a conclusion stating whether your hypothesis is true or not.

Name: _____

Queen Penelope Picks Out Clues

Queen, Penelope, Picks, Out, Clues

Q - **question**
P - **predict**
P - **plan/procedures**
O - **observe**
C - **conclusion**

Write a story using the following words: queen, Penelope, picks, out, clues, question, predict, procedures, plan, observe and conclusion.

_____

_____

_____

_____

_____

_____

_____

_____

_____

_____

_____

_____

_____

_____

_____

_____

_____

Queen Penelope Picks Out Clues (Cont'd)

Make illustrations for your story.

FORCE & MOTION

Name: _____

Make a list and draw a picture of all the things you can think of that push something.

Scientific Method

Name: _____

Make a list and draw a picture of all the things that you can think of that pull something.

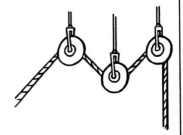

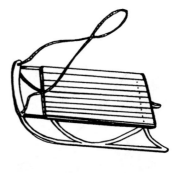

Venn Diagram

FORCE & MOTION

Name: _____

1. Place all the push things in one circle.

2. Place all the pull things in the other circle.

3. Place anything that can both push and pull in the middle cross over section.

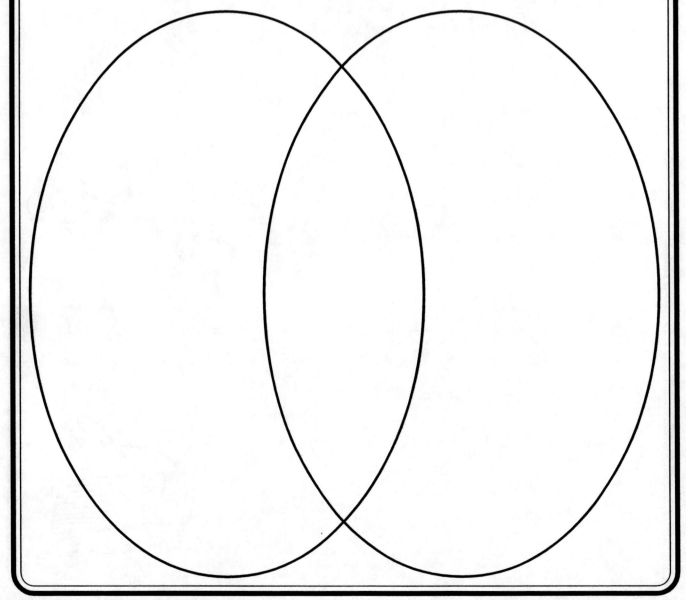

Vocabulary

Energy - there are many kinds of energy: human, potential, electrical, light and heat. Each kind of energy does work by moving molecules over a distance.

Force - something that changes the speed, direction or shape of an object by pushing or pulling.

Friction - this is the force that stops or slows something down when it comes in contact with that object.

Fulcrum - the still point of the turning world.

Gears - wheels that are found in machines; they have pieces (cogs) jutting out from them and hook into another wheel to make it spin.

Gravity - a force of attraction pulling objects together to various degrees.

Inertia - a word describing the condition of objects remaining as they are in motion or at rest unless a force acts upon them.

Kilogram - a unit of mass used in the metric system and the scientific community.

Lever - a solid length that can turn on a pivot point to move a force from one place to another.

Vocabulary

Lubricant - a substance that allows two surfaces to slide easily over one another.

Machine - something that does work for us by using forces.

Mass - the number of molecules in an object.

Motion - movement.

Potential energy - energy that is stored in an object when you prepare it to move and leave it to rest in this position.

Pulley - a simple machine made from a wheel that something can be wrapped around to make it easier to lift an object.

Speed - how fast an object covers a distance.

Weight - the force of gravity on an object pulling it towards the earth.

Windmill - a tower with large blades, which are pushed by the wind converting the movement of wind into the movement of molecules in the form of electricity.

Materials Required

Begin collecting materials well in advance of the unit, **or** send home this list of materials for the students to contribute to their learning.

1. Empty containers – plastic bottles, tubs, cartons, boxes of all sizes
2. String
3. Scissors
4. Glue
5. Wooden block shapes (cylinders, cubes, triangles etc...)
6. Paper clips
7. Elastic bands of various thickness and lengths
8. Rulers
9. Markers, pens, pencils and erasers
10. Unopened packaged items with their weight measured in milligrams on the outside of the package
11. Springs from old furniture
12. Old pans, paint buckets, pails
13. Old spools from thread
14. Toothpicks
15. Tape
16. Candles
17. Wire spirals from old notebooks
18. Thin straight sticks or dowels
19. Plastercene
20. Nuts (the metal sort)
21. Paper, cardboard of varying thickness, tracing paper, tissue paper
22. Pairs of things that are the same size and shape but different weights (i.e. a game die and a sugar cube or a golf ball and a ping-pong ball)
23. Plastic drinking cups
24. Coins or weights such as washers
25. Straws
26. Various small objects made of different materials such as a marble, pins and stones
27. Balloons
28. Stopwatches
29. Old carpet scraps
30. Soap
31. Plastic bags
32. Broom or mop handles (can come with broom and mop)
33. Baby powder
34. Wire coat hangers
35. Jar lids of various sizes
36. Corks

Identifying Method

FORCE & MOTION

Name: _____

Activity 1

1. Take the students to the gym.

2. Have them move around the space in a variety of directions.

3. On whistle commands, have them either start, stop or change directions (one whistle stop, two whistles start, and three whistles change directions – or any signals of your choice).

4. Have students complete the activity worksheet.

Question: How Do I Start, Stop and Change Direction?

I guess _____

_____

What I did _____

_____

What my senses told me _____

_____

It looked like this:

```



```

I learned _____

_____

Identifying Forces

Name: _____

Activity 1

Question: How Do you Stop?

Fill out the chart below:

How do I stop when I'm:	Explain in words	Draw a picture
Riding a bicycle?		
Ice skating?		
Roller blading?		
Running fast?		
In a car?		
Other?		

Identifying Forces

Name: _____

Activity 2

Explain what is happening in each of the pictures using the following words: magnetism, static electricity, muscular force and gravitational force:

_____
_____
_____
_____

_____
_____
_____

_____
_____
_____
_____

_____
_____
_____

Magnetism

Name: _____

Activity 1

Question: What is magnetism?

Color in all of the examples of magnetism on this page.

Static Electricity

Name: _____

Activity 1

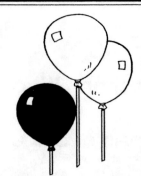

Question: What is Static Electricity?

Brainstorm a list of your senses.

Use your senses to describe what static electricity looks like in each of the following situations.

Object	Hear	See (draw (a picture)	Feel	Smell or Taste
Balloon				
T.V.				
Touching something after walking on a carpet				
Paper				
Clothes				

Electromagnetic Energy

FORCE & MOTION   Name: _____

Activity 1

Question: What's in a storm?

Make a web outlining all the things your senses pick up during a thunderstorm.

Muscular Force

Name: _____

Activity 1

Whenever our muscles shorten or lengthen, they do work. Sometimes our muscles can shorten without our body even moving at all. Try flexing your bicep (the muscle on the front and top of your arm) without moving your arm.

Can you think of ten examples of how your muscles work to help you each day?

1. _____

2. _____

3. _____

4. _____

5. _____

6. _____

7. _____

8. _____

9. _____

10. _____

Centripetal Force

Activity 1

Question: Does centripetal force increase, the faster an object spins around the center?

Materials required: arrange for the use of an open space such as a gymnasium, playground, playing field, courtyard or other open area.

Procedure:

1. Bring students into an area where they have space to move around.

2. Have students form groups of two or three.

3. Each joins one hand in the center (in even groups by shaking hands, in odd groups by grasping wrists). See diagram.

4. Have each group member place his or her right foot into the center of the circle with just the toe on the ground; at the same time, all group members pedal in a clockwise direction. See diagram.

5. Have the group spin at different speeds.

Conclusion:

The students will find that the faster they spin the greater the pull or centripetal force exerted on their arms.

FORCE & MOTION

Centripetal Force

Name: _____

Activity 2

Question: Does centripetal force increase the faster an object spins around a center?

I guess _____

_____

What I did _____

_____

What my senses told me _____

_____

It looked like this:

```



```

I learned: _____

_____

Centripetal Force

Activity 3

Question: Does centripetal force act on water?

Materials required:
- outside space (courtyard, playground or playing field)
- a bucket for each group (large ice cream bucket, margarine bucket, a paint tin, or any kind of bucket with a well attached handle)
- water

Procedure:

1. Half fill the bucket with water.

2. Move into an open space.

3. Place the bucket on the ground and do arm circles starting small and increasing in size to warm up the shoulder joint.

4. Pick up the bucket and hang onto the handle with your strongest arm.

5. Look around yourself and make sure you have a clear area.

6. Begin swinging the bucket 360 degrees (a full circle) around your shoulder like a ferris wheel.

7. After several swings, slow the bucket down and bring it to stillness at your side before putting it down on the ground.

8. Record your observations and clean up the investigation.

Conclusion:

Students will find that the water stays in the bucket even when it is on its side or upside down. While the bucket is spinning, the water is trying to go in a straight line but is being constantly stopped by the bottom of the bucket.

Afterthought: What would happen if you poked holes in the bottom of the bucket?

Plan your own investigation to determine if your prediction is correct.

(Note: This is a great Science Field Day Activity)

FORCE & MOTION

Name: _____

Activity 4

Question: Does centripetal force act on water?

I guess _____

_____

What I did _____

_____

What my senses told me _____

_____

It looked like this:

[ ]

I learned _____

_____

 **FORCE & MOTION**

Friction

Activity 1

Question: How does the roughness or smoothness of a surface affect how an object will move over it?

Materials required:
- a piece of cardboard
- desk tops or plastic trays
- an assortment of flat bottomed, non breakable objects such as a coin, an eraser, a pencil sharpener, and a game board piece
- ice cubes

Procedure:

1. Line your objects up along one end of the piece of cardboard.

2. Slowly tilt (by lifting) one end of the board until one or more of the objects begin to move.

3. Repeat steps 1-2 with the plastic or laminate surface (tray or desk).

4. Repeat steps 1-2 with the plastic or laminate surface but using the ice cube instead of the other objects.

Conclusion:

Students will notice that the smoother two surfaces are, the more easily they will slide across one another. Making a surface wet or ice covered is just about as slippery as it can get.

Afterthought: Why do elite competitive swimmers shave all of the hair off their bodies?

 **FORCE & MOTION**

Friction

Name: _____

Activity 2

Question: How does the roughness or smoothness of a surface affect how an object will move over it?

I guess _____

_____

What I did _____

_____

What my senses told me _____

_____

It looked like this:

```


```

I learned _____

_____

Gravity

Activity 1

Question: How does the weight of an object affect the pull of gravity upon it?

Materials required: - a collection of things that are the same size but different weights (i.e. golf ball/ping pong ball; a coin/a button; a book/an empty gift box)
- two aluminum pie plates or pans

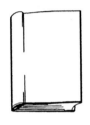 

Procedure:

1. Set up a chair with the aluminum pie plates placed on the ground, one on each side of the chair leg.

2. Have your partner pass you the paired objects.

3. Drop both objects from the same height at the same time, one on either side.

4. Listen for them to hit the pans and record which one hits first.

5. Repeat the experiment to see if the results are consistent.

Conclusion:

Students will observe that each pair lands at the same time. Gravity acts on objects with exactly the same force regardless of their weight.

Afterthought: What other factors might affect how gravity acts on an object?

 **FORCE & MOTION**

Gravity

Investigation 1

Design an experiment to test your ideas about gravity.

Student Investigation Topic _____

I guess _____

_____

What I did _____

_____

What my senses told me _____

_____

It looked like this:

[ ]

I learned _____

_____

Gravity

Name: _____

Activity 2

Question: How does the weight of an object affect the pull of gravity upon the object?

I guess _____

_____

What I did _____

_____

What my senses told me _____

_____

It looked like this:

$$\boxed{}$$

I learned _____

_____

Gravity

Activity 3

Question: How does surface area affect the speed that something will fall to the ground?

Materials required: two pieces of paper

Procedure:

1. Scrunch one of the two pieces of paper into a ball.

2. Drop both pieces of paper at the same time.

3. Record which piece of paper lands first.

Conclusion:

Students will observe that the paper ball lands more quickly than the flat piece of paper, although both weigh the same amount. The difference between the two is their surface area. The flat piece of paper needs to push more air out of the way in order to land than the paper ball.

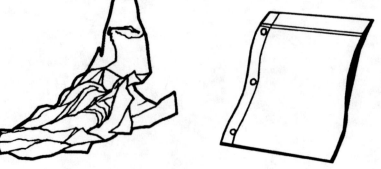

Afterthought: What are the two major forces acting on the paper as it falls?

 FORCE & MOTION

Gravity

Name: _____

Activity 4

Question: How does surface area affect the speed something will fall to the ground?

I guess _____

_____

What I did _____

_____

What my senses told me _____

_____

It looked like this

```


```

I learned: _____

_____

Magnetic Force

Activity 1

Question: Where is the magnetic north?

Materials Required: apple, tennis ball or other small ball

Procedures:

1. Imagine that the object (ball, apple etc.) is the earth spinning on its' axis.

2. Wrap your fingers around the outside of the object with your thumb sticking up.

3. Note which ever direction your thumb is facing is the magnetic north of the object.

4. Repeat steps 2 and 3, assuming the electons are going in a variety of directions.

Conclusion:

Students will observe the "Right Hand Rule". Electrons always move in a counter clockwise direction resulting in a magnetic field that is predictable by using your right hand. By wrapping your fingers in the direction that the electrons are traveling, your upward sticking thumb will point in the direction of the magnetic north for that object.

FORCE & MOTION

Magnetic Force

Name: _____

Activity 2

Question: Where is the magnetic north?

I guess _____

_____

What I did _____

_____

What my senses told me _____

_____

It looked like this:

[ ]

I learned _____

_____

Simple Machines

Activity 1

Question: How does the force needed to manually lift a load compare with the force required to lift a load with a simple machine?

Materials required: - three to five textbooks
- two pencils

Procedure:

1. Place the books on top of each other to form a stack.

2. Place your little finger under the bottom edge of the stack of books and attempt to lift the stack.

3. Put one pencil under the bottom edge of the stack of books.

4. Put the second pencil under the first one at ninety degrees to it and parallel to the book stack.

5. Push down on the end of the top pencil and attempt to lift the stack of books.

Conclusion:

Students will observe that it is difficult to lift the stack of books with their little finger, but easier to lift them with the pencils. The pencils are acting as a lever. The bottom pencil is acting as a fulcrum and the top pencil is acting as the lever arm. The further away from the place where you push down on the fulcrum, (the closer the bottom pencil to the stack of books) the easier it will be to lift the stack.

Simple Machines

Name: _____

Activity 2

Question: How does the force needed to manually lift a load compare with the force required to lift a load with a simple machine?

I guess _____

_____

What I did _____

_____

What my senses told me _____

_____

It looked like this:

```
┌─────────────────────────────────────────────┐
│                                             │
│                                             │
│                                             │
│                                             │
│                                             │
│                                             │
│                                             │
│                                             │
└─────────────────────────────────────────────┘
```

I learned _____

_____

 FORCE & MOTION

Transferring Energy

Activity 1

Question: What happens to a stationary object when hit by a moving object?

Task: Describe what happens, using the power of observation, when a stationary object comes into contact with a moving object.

Situation (example: a bowling ball hitting bowling pins)	Observation	Conclusions and further questions

 FORCE & MOTION

Kinetic Energy to Heat Energy

Investigation 1

Task: Observe the effect of friction on the temperature of an object.

Materials required: None

Procedure:

1. Place your hands on your face and note the temperature.

2. Rub your hands together and repeat step one above.

Conclusion:

Students will observe that friction results in an increase to temperature.

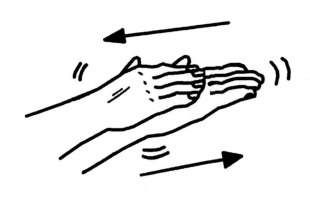

Kinetic Energy to Heat Energy

FORCE & MOTION   Name: _____

Investigation 2

Task: Observe the effect of friction on the temperature of an object.

I guess _____

_____

What I did _____

_____

What my senses told me _____

_____

It looked like this:

```
┌───────────────────────────────────────────────────┐
│                                                   │
│                                                   │
│                                                   │
│                                                   │
│                                                   │
│                                                   │
│                                                   │
│                                                   │
│                                                   │
└───────────────────────────────────────────────────┘
```

I learned _____

_____

Your Body in Motion

Name: _____

Activity 1

Complete the web with words describing how your body can move.

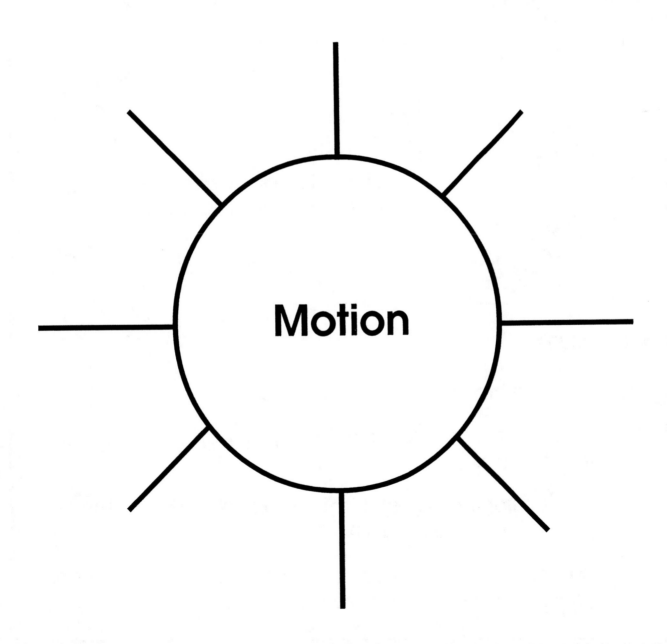

Motion

Magnets (Go Fish)

Activity 1

Question: What materials will a magnet pick up?

Materials required:
- a wooden rod or piece of dowling
- string
- paper
- tape
- small magnets
- a variety of small objects (paper clips, pencil sharpener, eraser, coins)

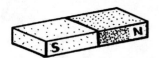

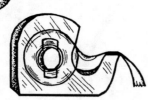
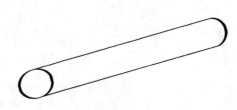

Procedure:

1. Tie the string onto the wooden rod.

2. Tape the magnet to a small scrap of paper and tape this to the string.

3. Place all of the objects into a make shift pool (garbage pail, area on the ground).

4. Fish for the objects observing and recording those that you can pick up and those that you cannot.

 FORCE & MOTION

Magnets (Go Fish)

Name: _____

Activity 2

I guess _____
_____

What I did _____
_____

What my senses told me _____
_____

It looked like this:

[blank box]

I learned _____
_____

Magnets (Go Fish)

Name: _____

Activity 3

Record the information you collect on this chart to show the results of your "Fishing" experiment.

  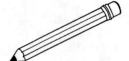 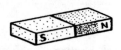

Object	Material	Pick up? yes or no

Forms of Energy

Name: _____

Activity 1

Identify the different forms of energy and suggest how they might be used to provide power to make something move.

Complete the chart for each of the forms of energy.

Kind of energy (Draw a picture)	How can this energy be used to move something?
emotional energy	
muscular energy	
potential energy	
wind energy	
solar energy	
hydro energy	
electric energy	
kinetic energy	
combustion energy	

Push & Pull

Activity 1

Question: What effect do the forces of push and pull have on objects?

Materials required:
- balls
- objects such as pencils, erasers, rulers, crayons,
- carpet squares or cloths
- desks

Procedure:

PART 1
1. Place one of the objects in the center of your desk.

2. Using your first finger (index finger), push the first object to the left, to the right, forward and backward.

3. Repeat all of the patterns above pulling the object instead of pushing it.

4. Record what you notice on the chart.

PART 2
1. Repeat the sequence with the second object, the third object etc.

PART 3
1. Repeat everything in Part 1 and 2 but first place the carpet square or piece of material on the desk.

FORCE & MOTION

Push & Pull

Name: _____

Activity _____

I guess _____
_____

What I did _____
_____

What my senses told me _____
_____

It looked like this:

```



```

I learned _____
_____

Activity 8

Question: Use the same finger to push your desk to the left.
What happens?

_____

_____

_____

_____

_____

_____

_____

Explain the difference between the results.

_____

_____

_____

_____

_____

_____

_____

_____

_____

Solving Problems with Forces

Name: _____

Activity 1

Complete the following chart.

Force	Problems/ challenges	Needs	Solutions	Questions
Example: Gravity	Things fall quickly to the ground and break.	If we can slow down the object's fall to the ground it won't hit as hard and it may not break.	We can increase the width of the object to try to make the object float down instead of fall.	How can we slow down an object being acted upon by gravity?
Static electricity				
Muscular force				
Magnetic force				
Gravity				
Other				

Solving Problems with Forces

FORCE & MOTION

Name: _____

Activity 2

Now make an experiment to test your solution to one of the problems you identified in the chart.

Problem: _____

_____

I guess: _____

_____

What I did: _____

_____

What my senses told me: _____

_____

It looked like this:

```
┌─────────────────────────────────────────────┐
│                                               │
│                                               │
│                                               │
│                                               │
│                                               │
│                                               │
│                                               │
└─────────────────────────────────────────────┘
```

I learned _____

_____

Windmill

Name: _____

Activity 2

Question: Can wind energy create movement?

I guess _____

_____

What I did _____

_____

What my senses told me _____

_____

It looked like this:

I learned _____

_____

Working with Forces

Activity 1

Question: What kinds of forces can I make with my hands?

Materials required: - modeling clay or plastercine

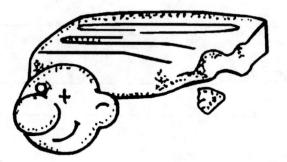

Procedure:

1. Play and explore, and record the movements you do and the actions they create.

Working with Forces

Name: _____

Activity 2

I guess _____

_____

What I did _____

_____

What my senses told me _____

_____

It looked like this:

[ ]

I learned _____

_____

Writing Instructions

Name: _____

Activity 1

Write out the instructions about how to make a windmill.

_____

_____

_____

_____

_____

_____

Draw the instructions.

```



```

How did you make your windmill unique?

_____

_____

_____

Present your windmill and its special features to the class.

Wind in the Windmills

Activity 1

Question: How does the speed that a windmill turns relate to the speed of wind acting upon it?

Materials required:
- fan
- windmill (see Activity 1 Windmill to make your own)
- stop watch or second hand of clock
- sticky notes

Procedure:

1. Mark one side of the windmill blade with a sticky note.

2. Turn on the fan to a low setting.

3. Time how long it takes for the windmill to make ten rotations.

4. Record your results.

5. Repeat with the fan on medium speed.

6. Repeat with the fan on high speed.

Wind in the Windmills

Name: _____

Activity 2

Question: How does the speed that a windmill turns relate to the speed of wind acting upon it?

I guess _____

_____

_____

What I did _____

_____

_____

What my senses told me _____

_____

_____

It looked like this:

_____
| |
| |
| |
| |
| |
| |
| |
|_____|

I learned _____

_____

_____

A Ballistic Balloon

Activity 1

Question: What force makes a balloon move forward when the air is coming out?

Materials required:
- string
- a piece of straw
- a long shaped balloon
- tape

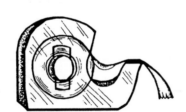

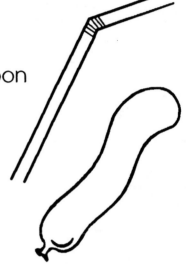

Procedure:

1. Put the string through the straw and tie both ends to chairs at the same height.

2. Blow up the balloon and hold the opening closed so no air comes out.

3. Get your partner to help you tape the balloon (blown up) to the straw.

4. Move the balloon towards one chair.

5. Let go of the end of the balloon; observe and record your results.

FORCE & MOTION

A Ballistic Balloon

Name: _____

Activity 2

Question: **What force makes a balloon move forward when the air is coming out?**

I guess _____

_____

What I did _____

_____

What my senses told me _____

_____

It looked like this:

_____
| |
| |
| |
| |
| |
| |
| |
| |
| |
| |
| |
|_____|

I learned _____

_____

Slippery Solutions

Activity 1

Indicate for each set of pictures, which picture is more slippery and which is less slippery.

1.

2.

3.

Identifying Forces

Name: _____

Investigation 1

Can you identify each of the following forces in the pictures? Use your vocabulary page to help you.

Air pressure, centripetal force, drag, friction, gravity, lift, magnetic force, buoyancy, life force.

Identifying Forces

Name: _____

Investigation 2

Can you identify each of the following forces in the pictures? Use your vocabulary page to help you.

Air pressure, centripetal force, drag, friction, gravity, lift, magnetic force, buoyancy, life force.

Name: _____

Investigation 3

Research how force and motion have been used by various cultures throughout the history of the world to do work.

Culture	How was force and motion used?	Picture
Ancient Egypt		
Medieval Europe		
Modern Day China		
Other		

Collage

Force and Motion Collage

Using old magazines, newspapers and computer clip art, find examples of things that relate to force or motion. Glue them onto a large piece of paper. Cut the paper out to make the shape of a simple machine. Give your collage a title.

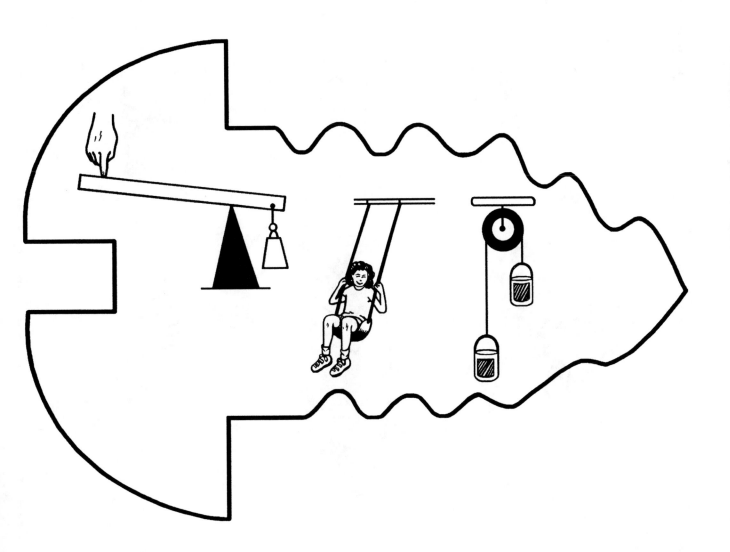

FORCE & MOTION
Learning Log

Name: _____

Learning Log

Force and Motion

Draw pictures of two things you have learned in this unit that surprised you.

FORCE & MOTION

Name: _____

Movement

1. What we did:

_____

_____

_____

_____

_____

_____

2. What I learned from this topic:

_____

_____

_____

_____

_____

_____

_____

3. What I would like to know next about this topic:

_____

_____

_____

_____

_____

_____

Centripetal Force

1. What we did:

_____

_____

_____

_____

_____

2. What I learned from this topic:

_____

_____

_____

_____

_____

3. What I would like to know next about this topic:

_____

_____

_____

_____

_____

Learning Log

Name: _____

Friction

1. What we did:

_____

_____

_____

_____

_____

_____

2. What I learned from this topic:

_____

_____

_____

_____

_____

_____

3. What I would like to know next about this topic:

_____

_____

_____

_____

_____

_____

Muscular Energy

1. What we did:

_____

_____

_____

_____

_____

_____

2. What I learned from this topic:

_____

_____

_____

_____

_____

3. What I would like to know next about this topic:

_____

_____

_____

_____

_____

 FORCE & MOTION

Learning Log

Name: _____

Gravity

1. What we did:

   _____
   _____
   _____
   _____
   _____
   _____

2. What I learned from this topic:

   _____
   _____
   _____
   _____
   _____
   _____

3. What I would like to know next about this topic:

   _____
   _____
   _____
   _____
   _____
   _____

Learning Log

Name: _____

Static Electricity

1. What we did:

_____

_____

_____

_____

_____

_____

2. What I learned from this topic:

_____

_____

_____

_____

_____

_____

3. What I would like to know next about this topic:

_____

_____

_____

_____

_____

_____

Learning Log

Name: _____

Magnetic Force

1. What we did:

_____

_____

_____

_____

_____

_____

2. What I learned from this topic:

_____

_____

_____

_____

_____

_____

3. What I would like to know next about this topic:

_____

_____

_____

_____

_____

_____

Learning Log

Name: _____

Circular to Linear Motion

1. What we did:

_____

_____

_____

_____

_____

_____

2. What I learned from this topic:

_____

_____

_____

_____

_____

_____

3. What I would like to know next about this topic:

_____

_____

_____

_____

_____

_____

Simple Machines

1. What we did:

_____

_____

_____

_____

_____

_____

2. What I learned from this topic:

_____

_____

_____

_____

_____

_____

3. What I would like to know next about this topic:

_____

_____

_____

_____

_____

_____

Conference

Name: _____   Date:_____

Activity Title	Rating 1, 2, 3, 4 1 - needs improvement 4 - meets and exceeds expectations				Comments
	1	2	3	4	
	1	2	3	4	
	1	2	3	4	
	1	2	3	4	
	1	2	3	4	
	1	2	3	4	
	1	2	3	4	
	1	2	3	4	
	1	2	3	4	
	1	2	3	4	
	1	2	3	4	
	1	2	3	4	
	1	2	3	4	
	1	2	3	4	
	1	2	3	4	
	1	2	3	4	
	1	2	3	4	
	1	2	3	4	
	1	2	3	4	
	1	2	3	4	

Evaluation

Topic : _____

Date : _____

Evaluation Marks:
S - Satisfactory
I - Improving
N - Needs Improvement
U - Unsatisfactory

Students' Names

FORCE & MOTION

Certificate

Excellence In Science Award

has successfully completed the unit on

FORCE & MOTION

Congratulations!

_____
Teacher

_____
Date

FORCE & MOTION

Vocabulary Meaning

FORCE & MOTION   Name: _____

gravity	fulcrum	inertia	energy	force
gears	kilogram	lever	machine	motion
mass	lubricant	potential energy		windmill
pulley	weight	speed		

_____ changes the speed, direction or shape of an object by pushing or pulling.

_____ is the force that stops something from moving (or really slows it down) when it comes in contact.

_____ is the still point of the turning world.

_____ There are many kinds of energy: human, potential, electrical, light and heat. Each kind of energy does work by moving molecules over a distance.

_____ Wheels that are found in machines; they have pieces (cogs) jutting out from them and hook into another wheel to make it spin.

_____ is a force of attraction pulling objects together to various degrees.

_____ is a word describing the condition of objects remaining as they are in motion or at rest unless a force acts upon them.

_____ is a unit of mass used in the metric system and the scientific community.

Vocabulary Meaning

_____ is a solid length that can turn on a pivot point to move a force from one place to another.

_____ is a substance that allows two surfaces to slide easily over one another.

A _____ is something that does work for us by using forces.

_____ is the number of molecules in an object.

_____ is another word for movement.

_____ energy is stored in an object when you prepare it to move and leave it to rest in this position.

A _____ is a simple machine made up of a wheel that something can be wrapped around to make it easier to lift an object.

_____ is how fast an object covers a distance.

_____ is the force of gravity on an object pulling it towards the earth.

A _____ is a tower with large blades, which are pushed by the wind converting the movement of wind into the movement of molecules in the form of electricity.

 FORCE & MOTION

Creative Writing

Ask each student to write an acrostic poem about an object that moves. Have them write the name of the object down the left hand side of the page and write words that describe it and how it moves (having each letter of the object start a descriptor word out across the page).

Example: **B**ouncing

                 Accelerating

                 Left and right

                 Laughter and fun

Name: _____   Date: _____

_____

_____

_____

_____

_____

_____

_____

_____

_____

_____

_____

_____

Creative Performing

Activity 1

Students will create an action performance in partners using words relating to force and motion. They can choose any six words, and then think of activities they can do with their bodies to demonstrate what the word means. Once they are organized, they can perform their "poetry in motion" for the rest of the class. One student can read the word out loud while the other student does the action that matches the word.

Next, choose one action poem to teach the whole class. Perform your action poems at an assembly or even a parents' night.

Partners' Names: _____

_____

Word	Action
1. _____	_____
2. _____	_____
3. _____	_____
4. _____	_____
5. _____	_____
6. _____	_____

Reading a Story

Name: _____

Activity 1

Each student can choose a story from the class library (a picture book or first chapter book will work best). After reading the story either with a buddy or on their own, each student will read the story a second time looking to find one example of force or motion in the book. Once they have found their example they can:

1. Draw a picture of the force or motion found.

2. Write a sentence underneath the picture describing what force or motion they think the picture represents.

3. If time allows, each student can tell about their story, show the picture they drew, and read their explanation of the force or motion found to the class.

Story Chosen: _____

Picture of force or motion found:

What I found: _____

_____

_____

_____

Word Web

Name: _____

Activity 1

Each student will create an idea web by writing or drawing as many things as they can think of when they read the words force and motion.

_____
_____
_____
_____
_____
_____
_____
_____
_____
_____
_____

 FORCE & MOTION

Listening for Force & Motion

Activity 1

Students will need: - a hard surface to write on (clip board, text book, writing folder)
- crayons, pencil crayons or pencils

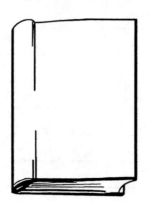

Instructions:

Each student will find a quiet place in the school or school yard under the supervision of their teacher.

Sit with this paper for 15 minutes without talking.

As you sit, draw or write down all of the sounds you hear.

After the time is up, return to your class and write beside each word or picture on your page the force or motion that it represents.

Formula Poetry

Name: _____

Activity 1

Create a poem using the following formula:

Line one: one noun (a person, place or thing)
Line two: two verbs (action words)
Line three: three verbs (action words)
Line four: four adverbs (words that describe the action words)
Line five: one verb (an action word)
Line six: one noun (a person, place or thing)

Example: Samantha
              Spinning, running
              Jumping, pushing, pulling
              Higher, harder, stronger
              Stop
              Samantha

Write your poem here:

_____

_____

_____

_____

_____

_____

_____

_____

_____

Rhyming Force & Motion

Name: _____

Activity 1

Can you think of words that rhyme with force and motion words?

Hint: You may need to make up a word of your own!

Word	Rhyming Words
Gravity	_____
Gears	_____
Mass	_____
Pulley	_____
Weight	_____
Lever	_____
Speed	_____
Force	_____
Windmill	_____
Motion	_____

Student Evaluation

Name: _____

What I liked best about this unit:

_____

_____

_____

_____

_____

_____

What was okay in this unit?

_____

_____

_____

_____

_____

_____

What I didn't like in this unit:

_____

_____

_____

_____

_____

_____

Thanks for your ideas!

Windmill Template

Cut out along solid line. Cut along dotted lines, stopping where they end.

Make windmills of different sizes from smaller or larger square sheets of paper.

(square 7" x 7")

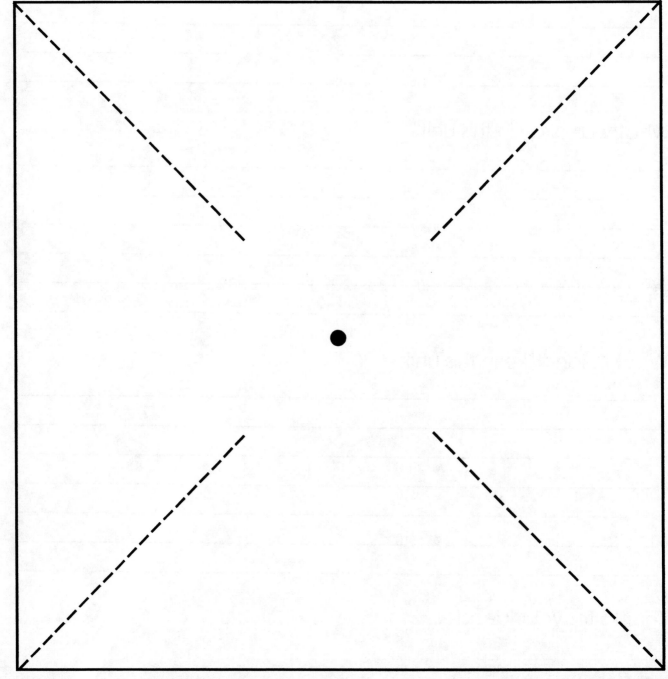

Publication Listing